EASY CONTEMPORARY PIECES

FOR SOLO PIANO

CHESTER MUSIC

Published by:
Chester Music Limited,
14-15 Berners Street, London W1T 3LJ, UK.

Exclusive Distributors:
Contact us:
Hal Leonard
7777 West Bluemound Road
Milwaukee, WI 53213
Email: info@halleonard.com

In Europe, contact:
Hal Leonard Europe Limited
42 Wigmore Street
Marylebone, London, W1U 2RY
Email: info@halleonardeurope.com

In Australia, contact:
Hal Leonard Australia Pty. Ltd.
4 Lentara Court
Cheltenham, Victoria, 3192 Australia
Email: info@halleonard.com.au

Order No. CH85349
ISBN 978-1-78558-430-5
This book © Copyright 2016 by Chester Music.

Compiled and edited by Sam Lung and James Welland.
Additional transcriptions and arrangements by Alistair Watson.
Music engraved and processed by Camden Music Services,
Paul Ewers Music Design, SEL Music Art Ltd and Sam Lung.
Cover designed by Tim Field.

Visit Hal Leonard Online at
www.halleonard.com

Printed in the EU.

CONTENTS

ABOUT THE PIECES...4

GEOFFREY BURGON A SENTIMENTAL WALTZ................6

NEIL COWLEY 2 YEARS..8

NEIL COWLEY TIGER MOTH.....................................10

NEIL COWLEY SHARD..15

PETER DICKINSON JUST A WALTZ............................18

LUDOVICO EINAUDI THE DARK BANK OF CLOUDS.............20

LUDOVICO EINAUDI QUESTA VOLTA........................25

LUDOVICO EINAUDI SARABANDE.............................30

NILS FRAHM FAMILIAR...33

PHILIP GLASS METAMORPHOSIS ONE......................39

PHILIP GLASS ETUDE No. 1......................................43

MORTON GOULD SLUMBER SONG..............................48

JOHN HARLE THREE SECRETS FROM THE ABYSS – No. 1 ...50

HAUSCHKA FRAGMENTS...52

HAUSCHKA BROOKLYN..54

BOWEN LIU MONOCHROME No. 1............................62

BOWEN LIU MONOCHROME No. 2............................64

PETER MAXWELL DAVIES SIX SECRET SONGS – No. 1 ...68

MICHAEL NYMAN CHATTERBOX WALTZ....................70

MICHAEL NYMAN THE EXCHANGE............................73

DUSTIN O'HALLORAN OPUS 28.................................76

DUSTIN O'HALLORAN OPUS 36.................................82

MAX RICHTER THE BLUE NOTEBOOKS.....................84

MAX RICHTER THE TARTU PIANO............................85

TERRY RILEY SIMONE'S LULLABY.............................59

GILES SWAYNE ZEBRA MUSIC – VI. WHITE ON WHITE.....88

KEVIN VOLANS ODE TO JOYCE................................90

SAM WATTS IMPROVISATION 1................................94

DEBBIE WISEMAN FORGIVE ME.................................92

ABOUT THE PIECES

GEOFFREY BURGON

A Sentimental Waltz

This short piece was published in 1998 as part of *Waiting*, a suite of nine easy pieces for piano, and dedicated to his wife, Canadian pianist and singer-songwriter Jacqueline Kroft.

NEIL COWLEY

2 Years
Shard
Tiger Moth

These three piano miniatures were written in 2016, and appear in this folio in their distilled form. More advanced pianists may feel comfortable elaborating the rich harmonies and taking liberty with the melodies, using varied rhythms and ornamentation.

PETER DICKINSON

Just A Waltz

This playful piece is the sixth movement from a suite entitled *Eight Very Easy Pieces For Piano*.

LUDOVICO EINAUDI

Questa Volta

Translated into English as 'this time', Questa Volta is the 11th track from Ludovico Einaudi's 2004 album *Una Mattina*.

The Dark Bank Of Clouds
AND **Sarabande**

These two pieces are from the critically-acclaimed 2013 album *In A Time Lapse*.

NILS FRAHM

Familiar

Nils Frahm titled his 2011 album *Felt*, referencing the technique of dampening the piano strings with material to suit night-time playing. The third track is presented here in an arrangement for easy piano by renowned pedagogue Hans-Günter Heumann.

PHILIP GLASS

Etude No. 1

This first etude is from Book 1 (Nos. 1–10), devised to explore a variety of tempi, textures and piano techniques, whilst also serving as a pedagogical tool for the composer's own piano playing.

Metamorphosis One

The first of a five-part work, 'Metamorphosis' refers to Franz Kafka's 1915 short story of the same name (*Die Verwandlung*). This piano work was released on the 1989 studio album *Solo Piano*.

MORTON GOULD

Slumber Song

This gentle piece is the fifth movement from Book 1 of Morton Gould's suite *At The Piano*.

JOHN HARLE

Three Secrets From The Abyss
I. With quiet simplicity, but intense introspection

This is the first of three short pieces for solo piano.

HAUSCHKA

Brooklyn

Part of Hauschka's *Small Pieces* this work was originally written for performance using prepared piano, requiring adhesive tape, screw caps, greaseproof paper and marbles, amongst other things. This piece is equally as effective on an unmodified instrument.

Fragments

This new piece is formed from fragmented recordings of Baroque-influenced keyboard improvisations, incorporating an initial texture reminiscent of a two-part invention, which is developed with dance rhythms and a flexible, modern approach to the harmony.

BOWEN LIU

Monochrome No. 1 AND Monochrome No. 2

These specially-written pieces maintain a sense of improvisation throughout, each naturally growing from motivic shapes and ostinati.

PETER MAXWELL DAVIES

Six Secret Songs – No. 1

This is the first in a set of six short pieces written in 1993 as a gift for a friend (a double bass player and composer from the BBC Philharmonic) who was celebrating the birth of his daughter.

MICHAEL NYMAN

Chatterbox Waltz
The Exchange

These pieces are adapted from Michael Nyman's scores to two films: The Chatterbox Waltz from 1995 Japanese anime Anne no Nikki (The Diary Of Anne Frank) and The Exchange from Michael Winterbottom's 2000 romance The Claim.

DUSTIN O'HALLORAN

Opus 28 AND Opus 36

Dustin O'Halloran began working on his first solo piano pieces whilst living in Italy, during a period of personal rediscovery with the piano. The composer describes the pieces as 'diary entries', capturing individual memories like small time capsules.

MAX RICHTER

The Blue Notebooks

Released in 2004, this tiny nocturne forms part of an album of 11 pieces, each building upon a particular motif.

The Tartu Piano

During a midwinter visit to the Estonian city of Tartu the composer found a particularly special piano within the brutalist concrete arts centre, and decided to write a piece dedicated to it.

TERRY RILEY

Simone's Lullaby

This intimate piece is the final movement from the piano suite The Heaven Ladder Book 7, written in 1994. An original version of the score has an indication to 'keep the soft pedal down throughout', and even if it's not used, this should be the effect. The indication to 'repeat until sleeping' should remind the performer to maintain the subdued soundscape throughout.

GILES SWAYNE

Zebra Music – No. 6 'White On White'

Giles Swayne's Zebra Music comprises twelve pieces written to be suitable for the junior contemporary piano student, offering new music ideas to younger players. As the title suggests, the music is written in 'layers' of black and white keys: one hand may be playing the black keys while the other hand plays the white; or both on black, or — in the case of this sixth piece — both on white.

KEVIN VOLANS

Ode To Joyce

This is included in a volume entitled Pint-Sized Piano Pieces, offering a selection of fun tunes varying in length and difficulty, each exploring a different aspect of piano technique.

SAM WATTS

Improvisation 1

As suggested by the title, this work should feel spontaneous — the melody emerges in the upper voice, halfway through the piece.

DEBBIE WISEMAN

Forgive Me

This piece was originally written for a BBC television adaptation of Hilary Mantel's Wolf Hall, set in Tudor England. Unusually, the composer chose to avoid pastiche music, opting for a more contemporary style.

A SENTIMENTAL WALTZ

MUSIC BY GEOFFREY BURGON

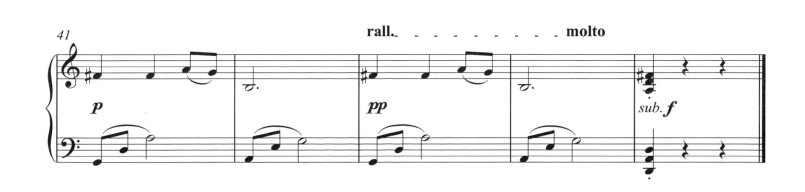

2 YEARS

MUSIC BY NEIL COWLEY

SHARD

MUSIC BY NEIL COWLEY

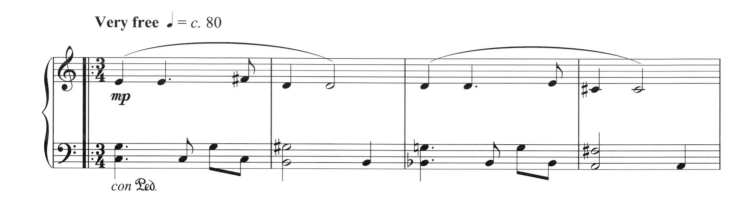

TIGER MOTH

MUSIC BY NEIL COWLEY

16

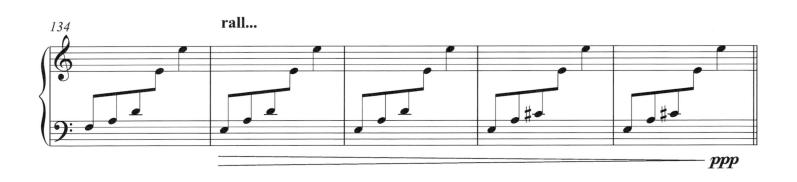

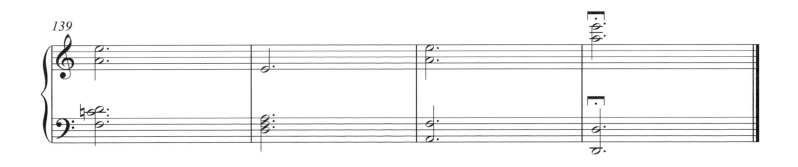

JUST A WALTZ

MUSIC BY PETER DICKINSON

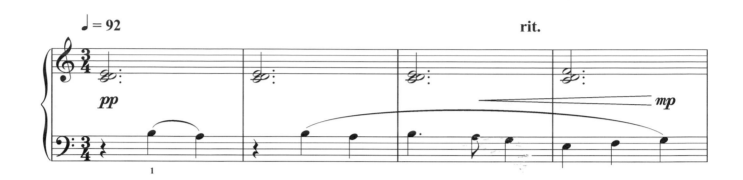

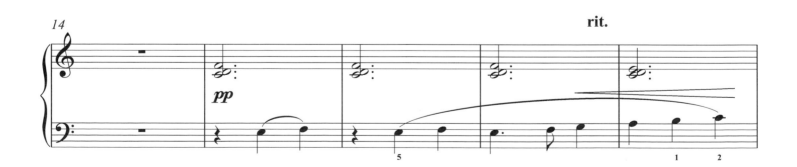

a tempo

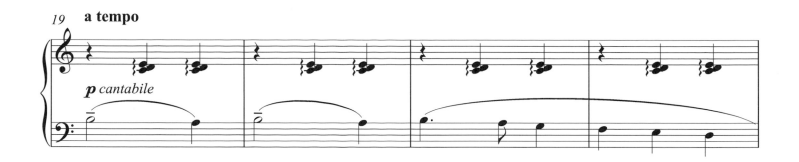

p cantabile

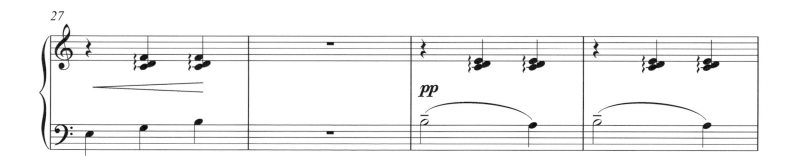

pp

19

THE DARK BANK OF CLOUDS

MUSIC BY LUDOVICO EINAUDI

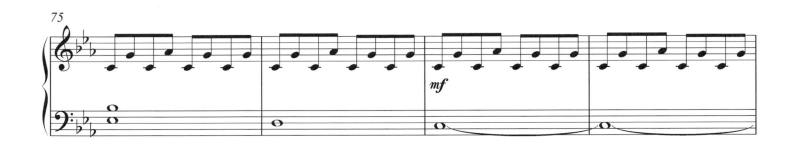

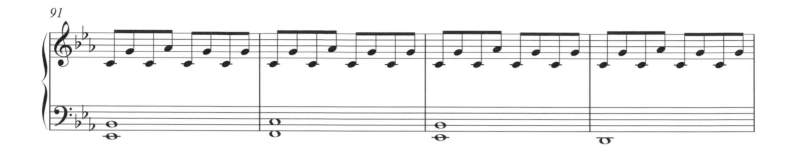

QUESTA VOLTA

MUSIC BY LUDOVICO EINAUDI

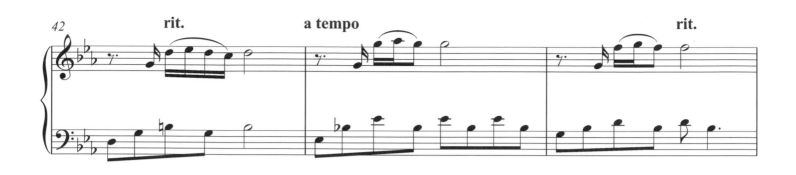

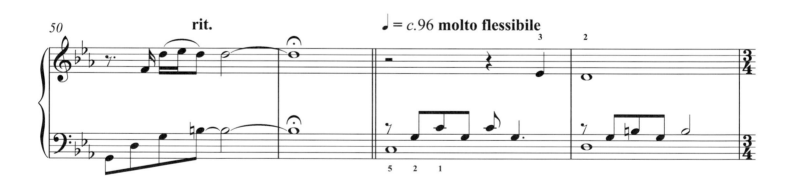

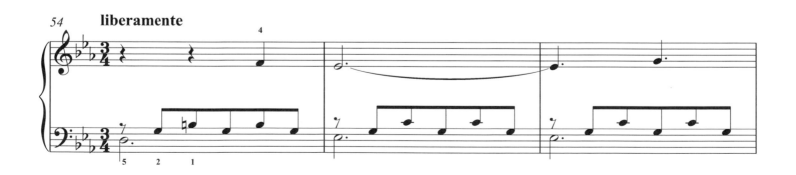

28

SARABANDE

MUSIC BY LUDOVICO EINAUDI

FAMILIAR

MUSIC BY NILS FRAHM

ARRANGED BY HANS-GÜNTER HEUMANN

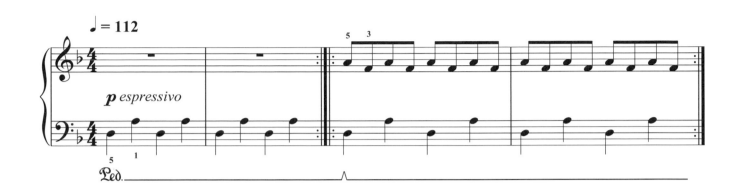

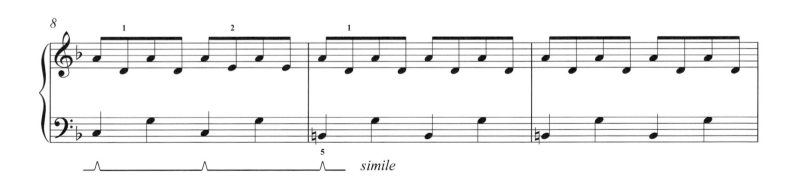

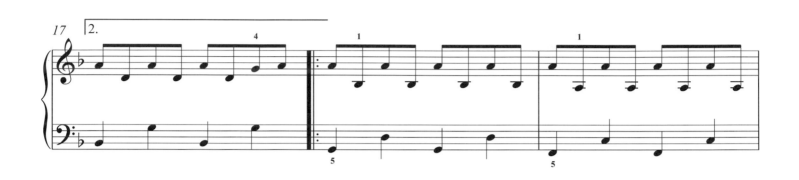

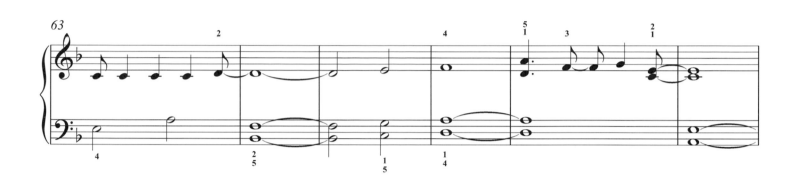

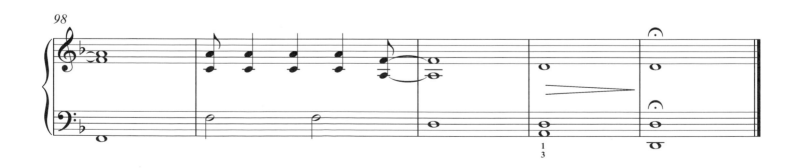

METAMORPHOSIS ONE

MUSIC BY PHILIP GLASS

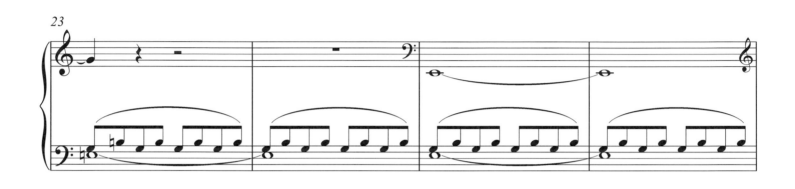

40

a tempo

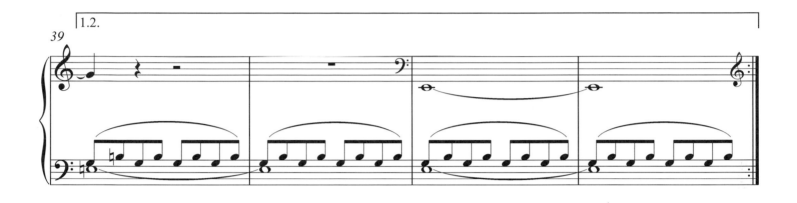

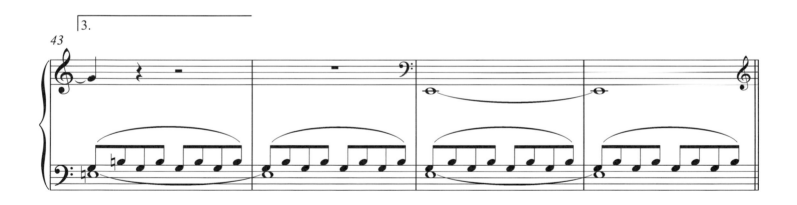

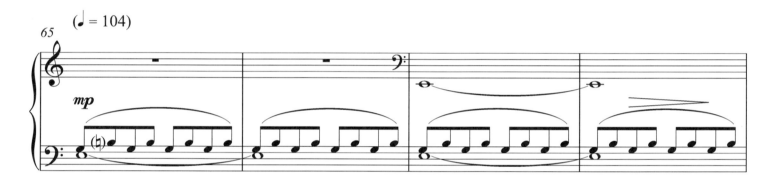

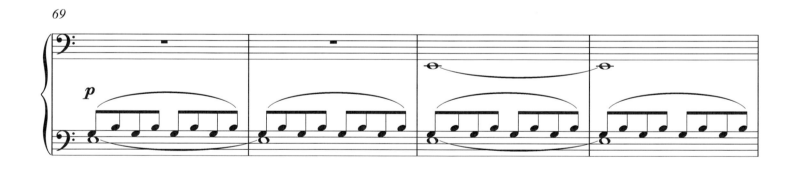

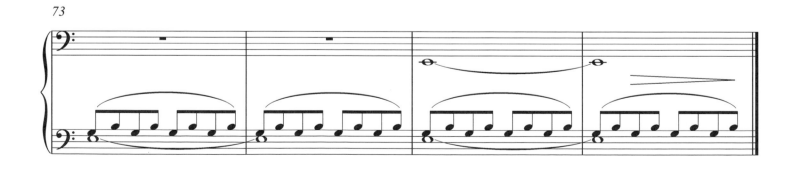

ETUDE No. 1

MUSIC BY PHILIP GLASS

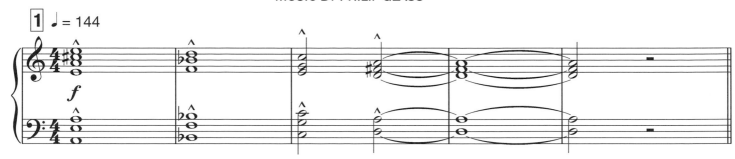

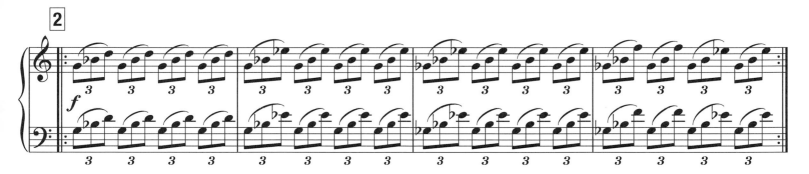

back to Fig. 2
(with repeats)

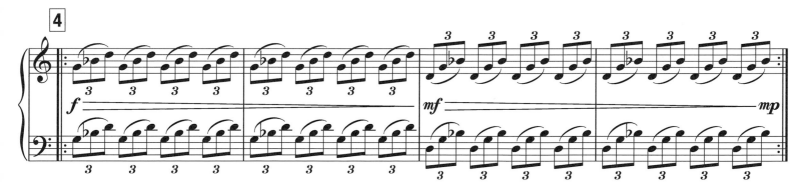

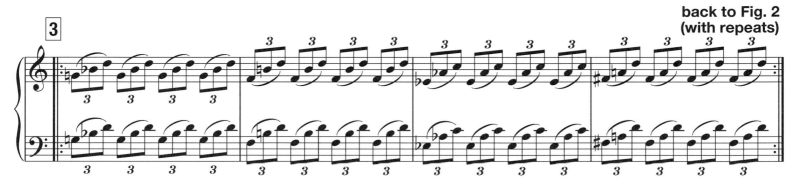

back to Fig. 7
(with repeats)

44

back to Fig. 14
(with repeats)

45

back to Fig. 21 (with repeats)

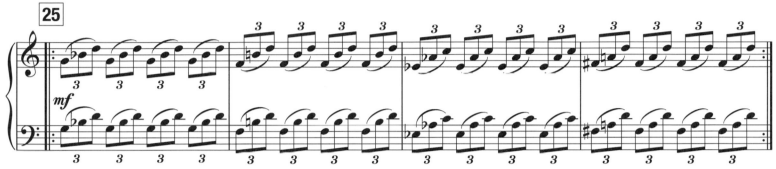

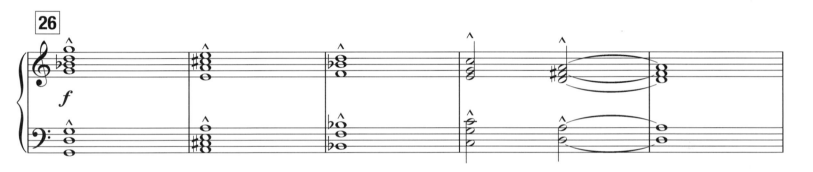

27 A little slower

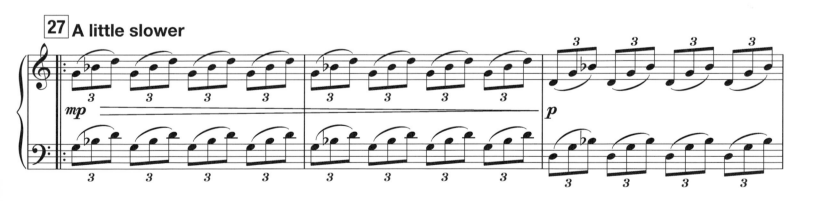

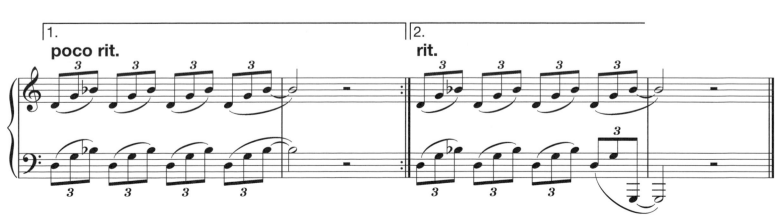

SLUMBER SONG

MUSIC BY MORTON GOULD

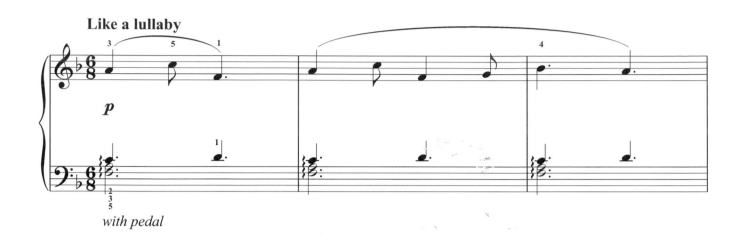

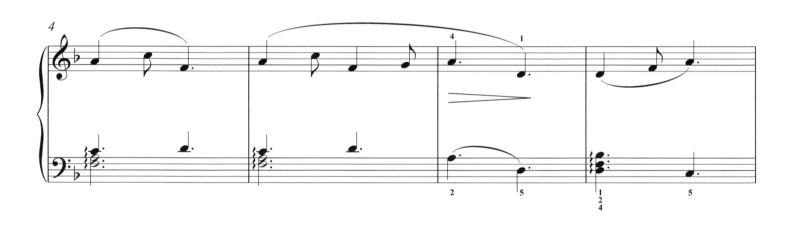

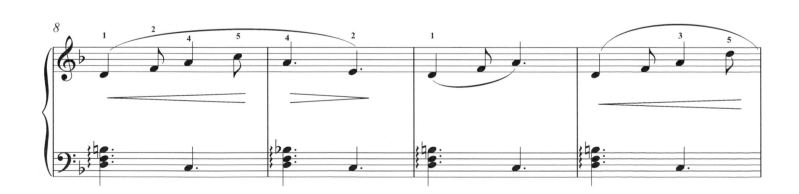

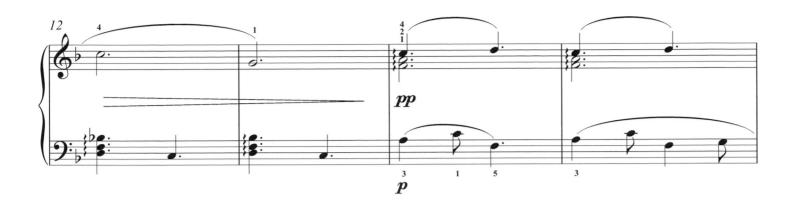

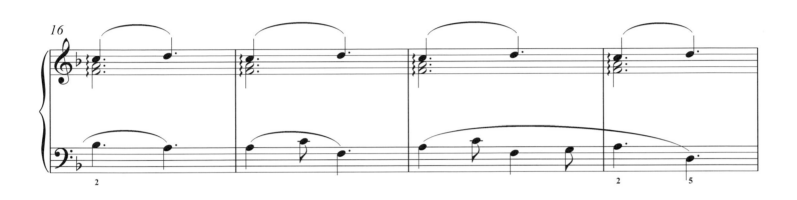

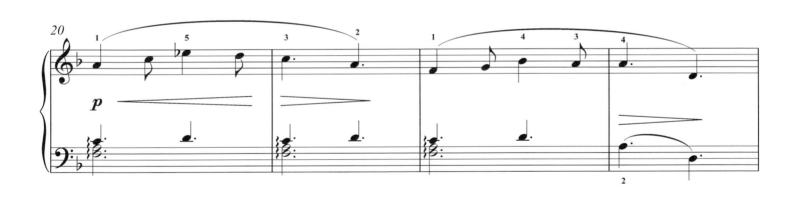

(Sleep,   sleep,   sleep.)

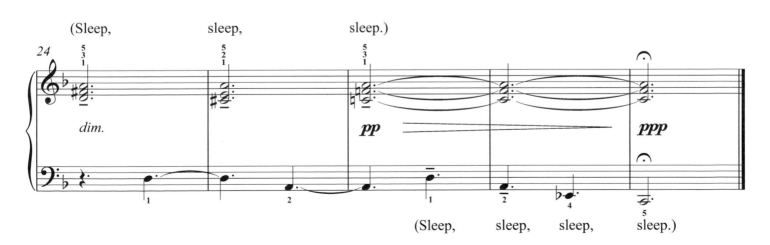

(Sleep,   sleep,   sleep,   sleep.)

THREE SECRETS FROM THE ABYSS

No. 1

MUSIC BY JOHN HARLE

With quiet simplicity, but intense introspection ♩ = *c.*62

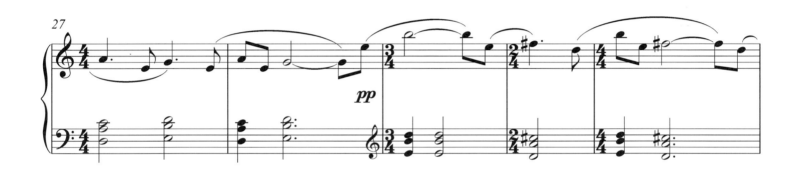

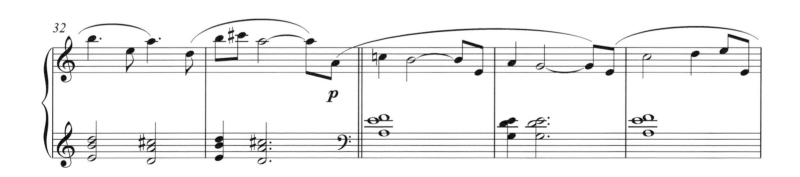

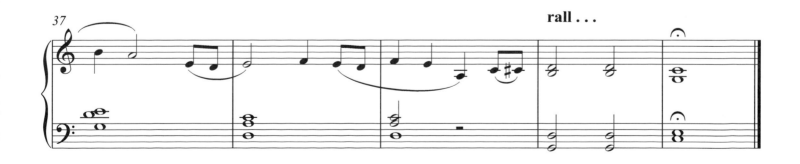

FRAGMENTS

MUSIC BY HAUSCHKA

BROOKLYN

MUSIC BY HAUSCHKA

2

SIMONE'S LULLABY

MUSIC BY TERRY RILEY

una corda throughout, Ped. as needed

MONOCHROME No. 1

MUSIC BY BOWEN LIU

MONOCHROME No. 2

MUSIC BY BOWEN LIU

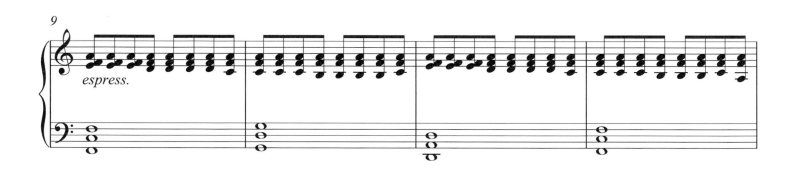

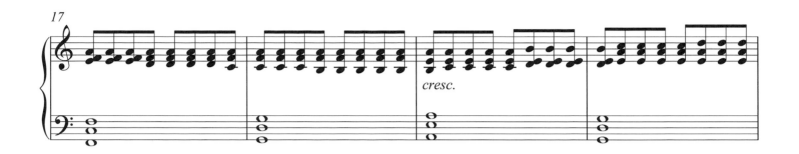

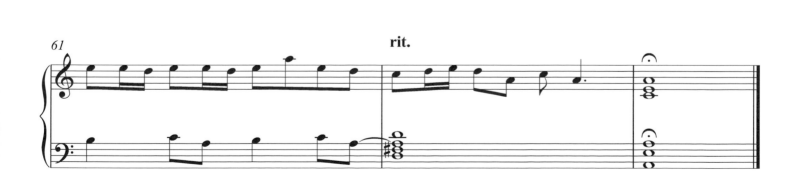

SIX SECRET SONGS

No. 1

MUSIC BY PETER MAXWELL DAVIES

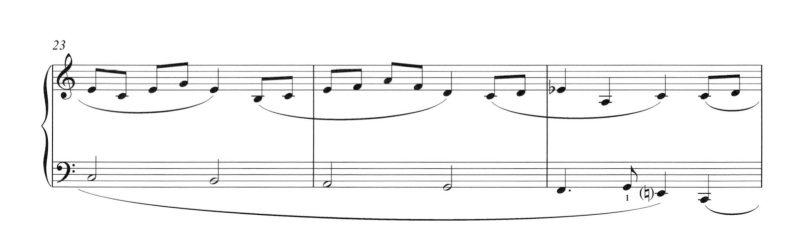

CHATTERBOX WALTZ

MUSIC BY MICHAEL NYMAN

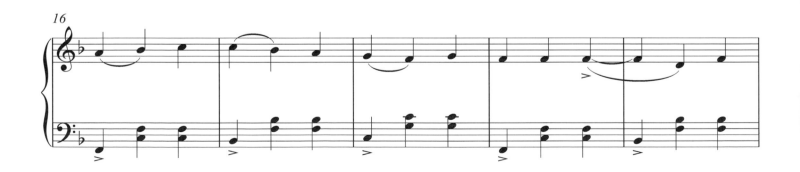

71

72

THE EXCHANGE

MUSIC BY MICHAEL NYMAN

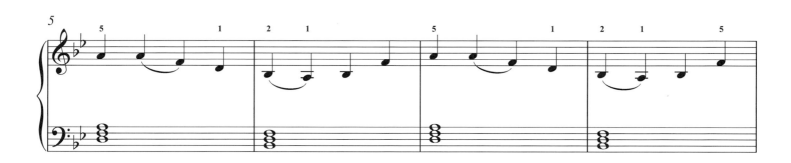

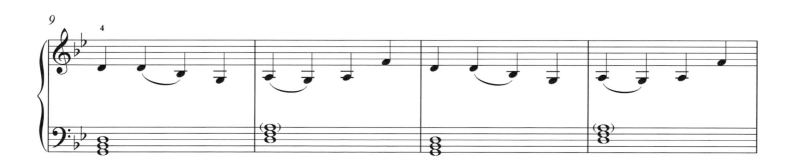

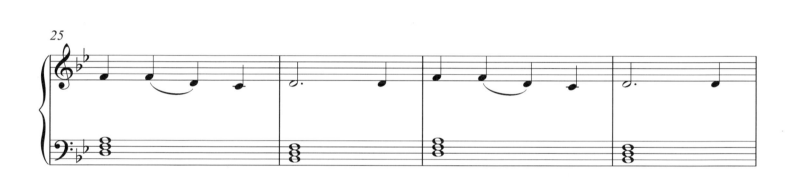

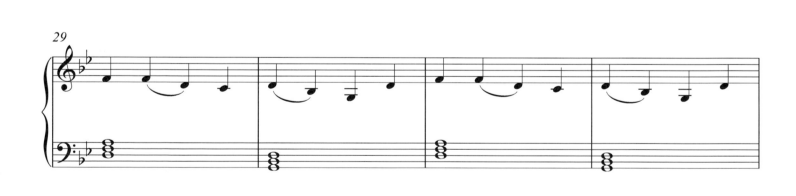

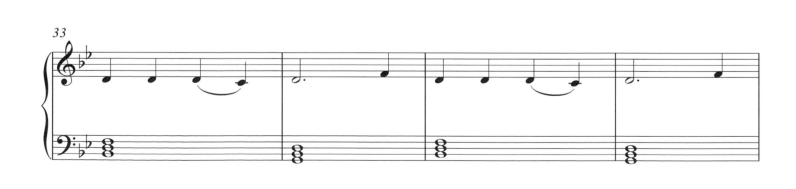

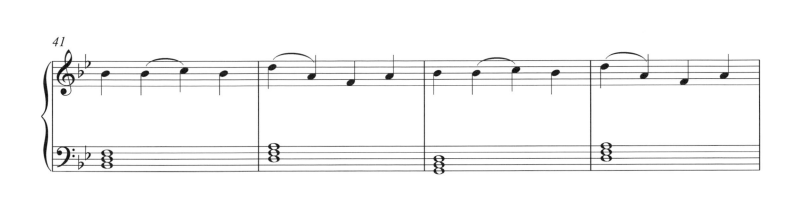

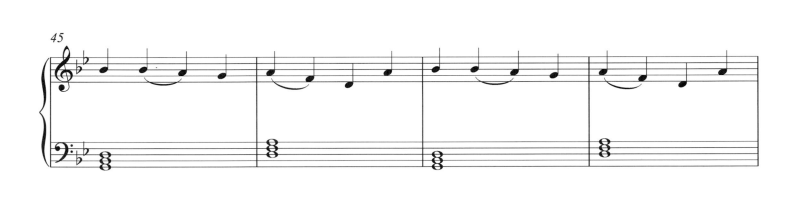

OPUS 28

MUSIC BY DUSTIN O'HALLORAN

rit.

81

OPUS 36

MUSIC BY DUSTIN O'HALLORAN

poco rit.

a tempo   rit.

rit.

83

THE BLUE NOTEBOOKS

MUSIC BY MAX RICHTER

THE TARTU PIANO

MUSIC BY MAX RICHTER

ZEBRA MUSIC

No. 6 – WHITE ON WHITE

MUSIC BY GILES SWAYNE

ODE TO JOYCE

MUSIC BY KEVIN VOLANS

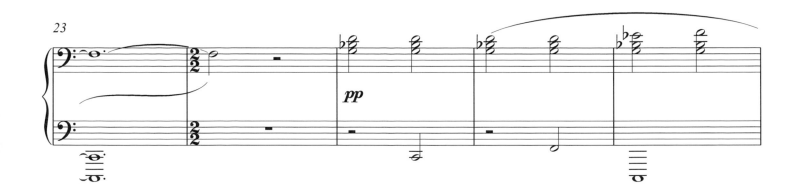

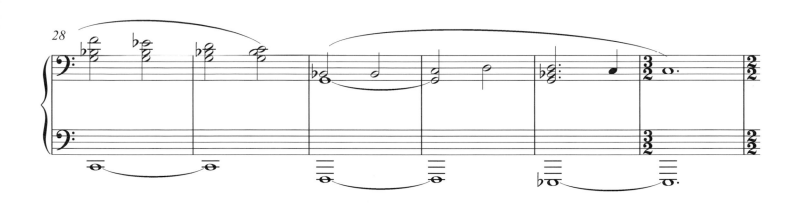

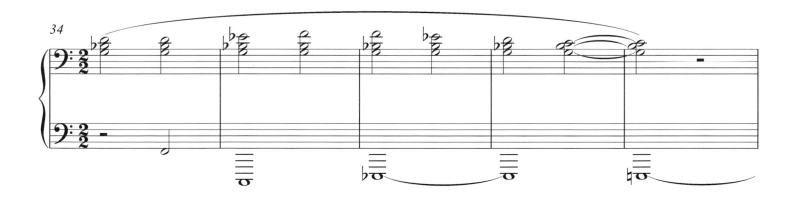

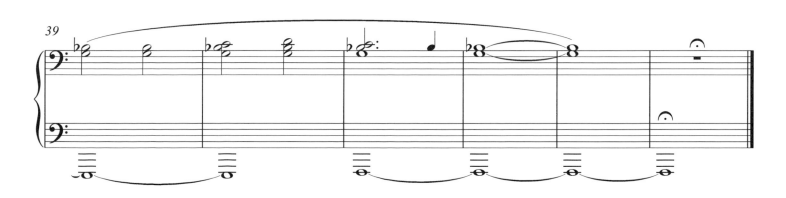

FORGIVE ME

MUSIC BY DEBBIE WISEMAN

IMPROVISATION 1

MUSIC BY SAM WATTS